DP8

Park

Jen Green

Photographs by Emma Solley

WAYLAND

First published in 2010 by Wayland

Copyright © Wayland 2010

Wayland
338 Euston Road
London NW1 3BH

Wayland Australia
Level 17/207 Kent Street
Sydney, NSW 2000

Senior editor: Camilla Lloyd
Designer: Phipps Design
Photographer: Emma Solley
Illustrator: Peter Bull

Picture Acknowledgments:
The author and publisher would like to thank the following for allowing their
pictures to be reproduced in this publication:
p.10 Robert Pickett/CORBIS; p.18 Brooke Whatnall Shutterstock;
p.24 Joseph Calev Shutterstock; p.25 Graeme Purdy/iStockphoto;
p.27 (bottom) Jamie Harron Papilio/CORBIS.

British Library Cataloguing in Publication Data:
Green, Jen.
 Park. – (Nature trail)
 1. Urban ecology (Biology)–Juvenile literature.
 2. Parks–Juvenile literature.
 I. Title II. Series
 577.5'5-dc22

ISBN: 978 0 7502 6094 7

Printed in China

Wayland is a division of Hachette Children's Books, an Hachette UK company.
www.hachette.co.uk

Contents

In the park

Parks are green spaces, usually in built-up areas such as towns and cities. Some parks are huge, others are tiny. Big or small, parks provide a wild space for plants and animals. That's why parks are great places to study nature!

Parks contain hundreds of different plants and animals, which you can discover if you look closely.

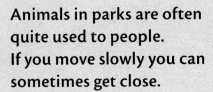

Animals in parks are often quite used to people. If you move slowly you can sometimes get close.

This symbol warns when special care is needed. Wash your hands after touching soil. Always take good care of nature. Never pick plants, and disturb animals as little as possible.

On the trail

On the nature trail you will need warm, waterproof clothing, strong shoes, a hat and sun cream.

hat

waterproof clothing

strong shoes or boots

sun cream

Make notes and drawings using a notebook, pen and coloured pencils. A magnifying glass, binoculars and a collecting jar will be useful.

collecting jar

coloured pencils

notebook and pen

magnifying glass

binoculars

Places to live

A **habitat** is a particular place where plants and animals live, such as a forest, lake or meadow. Parks have different areas such as lawns, ponds, flowerbeds and woodlands. Each is like a mini-habitat with its own set of plants and animals.

Some parks have lawns and meadows. Dandelions are growing in this meadow.

What do you see?

The main things you need to explore nature are your senses and a little patience. Take time to look and listen carefully. Be aware of smells and sounds. Keep still and quiet, so you don't scare animals away.

These Canada geese live on the banks of the lake where they can find food.

Bees and butterflies can be found near flowerbeds. Minibeasts shelter under stones.

Changing seasons

The park constantly changes as the weather gets warmer or colder. We call these changes the seasons. Plants and animals live their lives according to the yearly pattern of spring, summer, autumn and winter. That means there's always something new to see in the park!

Winter is the coldest season.
Lakes freeze over and snow may fall.
Many trees have no leaves.
Some animals spend winter asleep.

What do you see?

Start to record what you see in different seasons. Write down the date and weather. Try to identify the plants and animals you see. Record what animals are doing. Draw or photograph what you see.

8

In spring the weather warms up. Trees and plants grow new leaves and blossoms. Birds build nests and lay their eggs. Young animals are born.

Summer is the warmest season. Leafy trees provide shade. Birds such as swans, and other animals rear their young. Insects fly about.

In autumn the weather gets colder. Leaves turn yellow and fall from trees. Animals such as squirrels prepare for winter by burying nuts.

Which is your favourite season in the park?

In the grass

Grassy lawns make great hiding places for wildflowers, insects and other minibeasts. Worms, beetles and ants live in the soil. To a small creature such as an ant, the lawn is a towering jungle of green stalks, leaves and flowers.

Worms tunnel through the mud. They swallow soil and bits of plants.

Daisies open their petals by day and shut at night. The word daisy is short for 'day's eye'.

What do you see?

Ants scurry about finding food to take back to the nest. A long line of ants forms between the nest and the food. Follow the ant trail. Draw a map of the ants' route. What food have they found?

These ants are feeding on a dead insect.

Ants may be red, black or yellow. What colour are the ones you found?

In the trees

Trees in the park provide shade and a home for animals such as birds, squirrels and insects. Trees spread their leaves high in the air. The trunk supports the tree. The roots spread underground, gathering water.

Different **species** of trees have different shapes. Here are some common trees found in parks.

Oaks (right) and chestnuts (below) have a rounded shape.

Fir trees have a triangular shape.

Poplars are tall and slender.

Many different animals live in a big tree such as an oak, high on twigs and branches, on the bark or among the roots.

Trees have leaves of different shapes. This can help you identify the tree. These are oak leaves.

How many leaf shapes can you find?

What do you see?

Look for birds, squirrels and butterflies high in trees using binoculars. What do you think the animals were doing? Can you identify the species you see?

Blackbirds are common woodland birds that sometimes nest in parks.

In a bush

Bushes and **shrubs** are smaller than trees, but have the same features: leaves, twigs, roots and a woody stem. In spring and summer, all sorts of minibeasts make their homes in bushes. Some feed on leaves, while others hunt other minibeasts!

Leaves have lines called **veins** spreading out from the centre. Veins carry food and water around the leaf.

These are some common minibeasts found in bushes.

Caterpillars are young moths or butterflies.

Aphids (right) and shield bugs (below) suck plant sap.

Bark beetles eat leaves. Their young eat wood.

How many different minibeasts can you find?

Spiders spin their webs in bushes to catch **prey** such as flies.

What do you see?

Investigate the minibeasts that live on a bush. Spread a sheet or tablecloth under the bush. Gently shake a branch and see what lands on the sheet. Look at your finds using a magnifying glass. Put the creatures back gently when you have finished.

Butterflies visit buddleia flowers to sip sugary **nectar**.

By the water

Water in a park includes lakes, ponds and birdbaths. Many living things are found by water. As well as plants such as reeds and lilies, there are waterbirds, dragonflies, fish and frogs.

Dragonflies grow up underwater. The adult insects live on land and hunt for food while flying.

These waterbirds are common in parks.

A moorhen has a red beak.

A coot has a white patch above the bill.

This gull has a black head.

⚠ Be careful near water. Don't get too close to the edge!

The feathers of the male mallard ducks are colourful.

What do you see?

Look for waterbirds using your binoculars. Ducks, swans, geese and gulls swim in open water. Coots and moorhens lurk around the edge. Can you identify the birds you see?

Female mallard ducks are not as brightly coloured as the males.

Can you spot what the waterbirds are doing?

Under a stone

All sorts of minibeasts live under stones and in damp corners. Counting their legs can help you identify them. Insects such as beetles and earwigs have six legs. Spiders have eight legs. Centipedes, millipedes and woodlice have many legs. Slugs, snails and worms are legless.

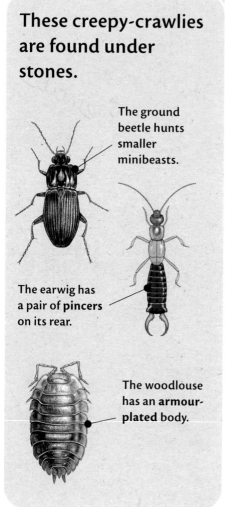

These creepy-crawlies are found under stones.

The ground beetle hunts smaller minibeasts.

The earwig has a pair of pincers on its rear.

The woodlouse has an armour-plated body.

This is a centipede.

What do you see?

Turn over a stone carefully to see what minibeasts live beneath. Count the legs.

⚠ Centipedes can nip you with their fangs. Wash your hands after touching soil.

The snail's shell protects its soft body.

Slugs are similar to snails but have no shell.

How can you tell the difference between slugs and snails?

19

Flowers

Flowers brighten up the park and provide food for insects. Their sweet scents and bright colours attract bees and butterflies. As insects fly between flowers, they transfer dusty **pollen**. This allows flowers to make seeds, so new plants can grow.

Flowers have different shapes and colours, but all have the same parts: a stem, petals, and long stalks called stamens that produce pollen.

What do you see?

Try drawing the flowers you see. First study the flower's shape. Some flowers are flat or rounded, others are shaped like stars or bells. Add colour with pencils or pens.

petal

stamens with pollen grains

stem

Bees visit flowers to sip nectar. The bee's body is dusted with pollen, which rubs off on the next flower it visits. This allows the second flower to make seeds.

What insects do you see visiting flowers?

Flowers bloom at different times of year.

Crocuses bloom in spring.

Irises bloom in summer.

Pansies can bloom in spring, summer, autumn or winter.

Tulips bloom in spring. Their cup-shaped flowers open by day and close at night.

21

Life cycles

If you visit the park often, you will see small changes taking place from day to day. In just a few days, flowers bloom, then drop their petals and make seeds. In a short few weeks, young insects hatch from eggs and grow into adults. These changes are part of life cycles.

Weeds called dandelions have a speedy life cycle. In just a day or two, the flower opens, blooms and dies.

After the flower dies winged seeds form. The wind blows the seeds away.

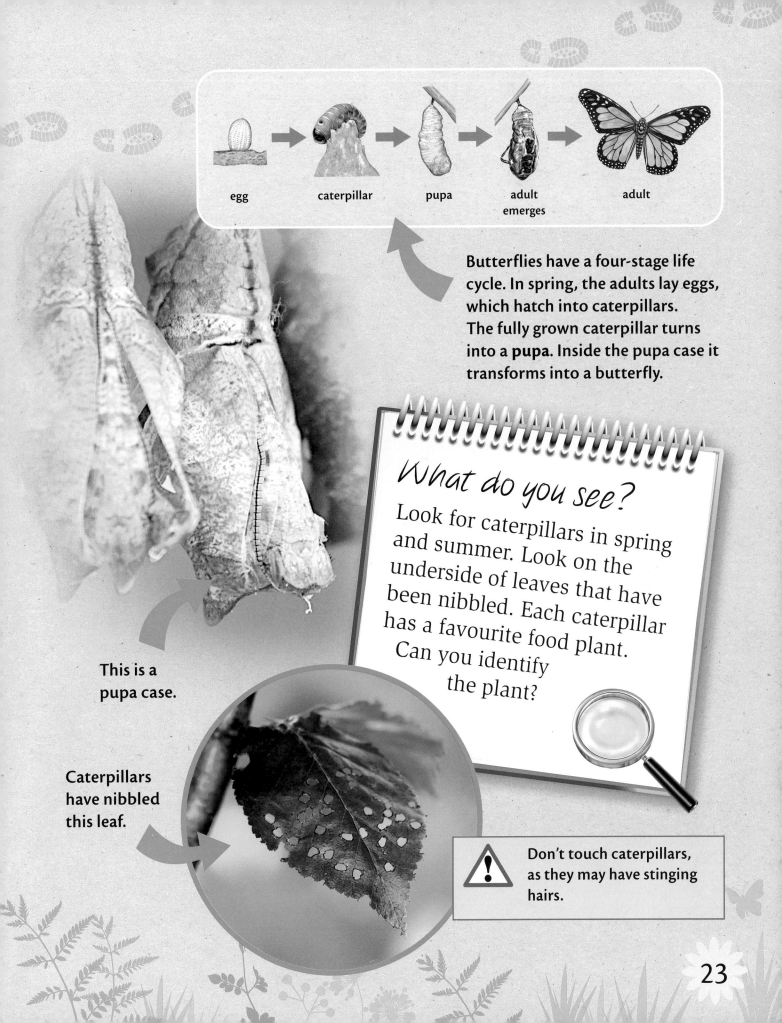

egg → caterpillar → pupa → adult emerges → adult

Butterflies have a four-stage life cycle. In spring, the adults lay eggs, which hatch into caterpillars. The fully grown caterpillar turns into a **pupa**. Inside the pupa case it transforms into a butterfly.

What do you see?

Look for caterpillars in spring and summer. Look on the underside of leaves that have been nibbled. Each caterpillar has a favourite food plant. Can you identify the plant?

This is a pupa case.

Caterpillars have nibbled this leaf.

Don't touch caterpillars, as they may have stinging hairs.

23

Food chains

Living things in the park form a web of life. The links between them can be shown in diagrams called food chains. Plants are at the base of most food chains. They make their own food using sunlight energy and minerals from the soil. Plants provide food for animals called **herbivores**. These are hunted by meat-eating **predators**.

This food chain shows the links between the ladybird, aphid and rose. The ladybird is at the top of this little chain.

Aphids are often found on roses. Ladybirds hunt aphids, which helps to save the flowers!

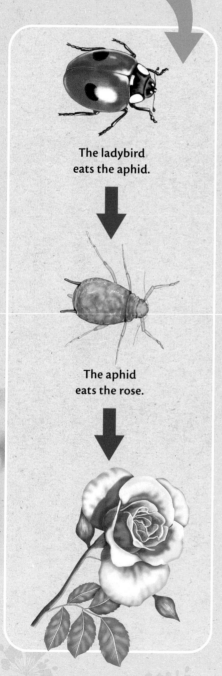

The ladybird eats the aphid.

The aphid eats the rose.

This robin is eating a
mealworm – a young
beetle. Mealworms feed
on young plants.

What do you see?

Draw a food chain showing
the robin, mealworm and
plants. Now try drawing other
simple food chains that you
see in the park. You will
need to know what each
animal eats.

Through the day

Animals in the park follow a daily rhythm. Some are out and about by day, like humans. Others search for food at dawn, dusk, or at night. For example, butterflies gather nectar in early morning. Most birds look for food by day. Moths and bats fly at night.

Squirrels are active by day, looking for nuts, seeds and fruit.

Birds sing at dawn. This is called the dawn chorus.

What do you see?

Visit the park at different times of day – for example in the early morning, at midday and dusk. Record the animals that are active in trees, on the grass and by the lake.

Shy animals such as foxes, mice and this hedgehog look for food in the dark.

Nature diary

Build up a picture of life in the park through the year by keeping a nature diary. A guidebook to local wildlife can help you identify plants and animals. You could make a collection of finds such as leaves and feathers, or draw a map of the park.

KEEP NOTES

Always take your notebook with you. Record the date, time of day, weather and the exact **location**. Describe what animals are doing. You could add drawings, photos, or even samples such as leaves.

Do you recognise this insect?

Date: 26 May

Time: 9 am

Weather: Sunny

Location: Green Park by the lake

Observations: Saw a mallard with her duckling.

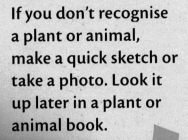

You could make a collection of leaves, nuts, seeds and feathers.

If you don't recognise a plant or animal, make a quick sketch or take a photo. Look it up later in a plant or animal book.

TOP TIPS

● Don't forget to keep still and quiet when you go nature-spotting.

● Don't let your shadow fall on animals such as insects.

● Approach animals with the wind blowing towards you so they don't catch your scent.

MAKE A MAP

Make a map of the park showing mini-habitats such as trees, lawns, wild areas, lakes, flowerbeds and rockeries. Show paths and buildings too.

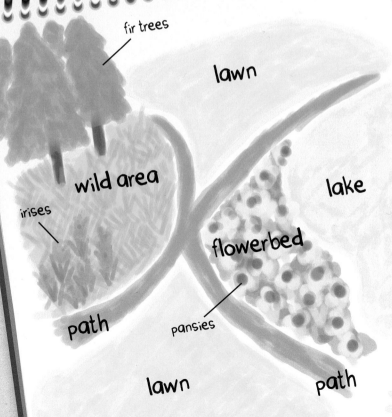

fir trees

lawn

wild area

irises

lake

flowerbed

path

pansies

lawn

path

Glossary

armour-plated When an insect or animal has a hard, protective shell.

bloom When flowering plants come into flower. This usually happens in the spring or summer.

bush A woody plant that is smaller than a tree.

habitat The natural home of a plant or animal, such as a wood, meadow or the seashore.

herbivore An animal that eats plants.

location A place.

nectar A sweet, sugary liquid produced by flowers to attract insects.

pincers Moveable parts of some insects that are used to pick up and carry things.

pollen Yellow grains produced by flowers in order to make seeds.

predator An animal that hunts other animals for food.

prey An animal that is hunted by another.

pupa The third stage in the life cycle of a moth or butterfly, before it becomes an adult.

shrub A woody plant that is smaller than a tree.

species A particular type of plant or animal, such as an oak tree or a tortoiseshell butterfly.

stamens The long stalks in the middle of a flower that produce pollen.

veins Lines that run through leaves, supplying water and food.

Further information

BOOKS

Look around you: Countryside
by Ruth Thomson, Wayland, 2007

Animal Neighbours series
by Michael Leach, Wayland, 2007

The Mud Pack: Wildlife
by James Parry, The National Trust, 2002

WEBSITES

www.bbc.co.uk/nature/animals/
The BBC's science and nature website is packed with facts about birds, mammals and other wildlife.

www.bbc.co.uk/springwatch/
www.bbc.co.uk/autumnwatch/
The BBC's Springwatch and Autumnwatch sites have information about exploring the natural world.

www.animal.discovery.com/ animals/
The Animal Planet website has information, pictures and videos about all kinds of wild animals.

Index

Nature Trail

Contents of titles in the series:

WAYLAND